Williamson  Publishing

Be A Clown!

Techniques from a Real Clown

Ron Burgess
aka "Silly Willy"

Illustrations by Heather Barberie

Quick Starts for Kids!™

WILLIAMSON PUBLISHING • CHARLOTTE, VERMONT

Library of Congress Cataloging-in-Publication Data

Burgess, Ron.
    Be a clown! : techniques from a real clown! / Ron Burgess, aka "Silly Willy."
        p. cm. — (Quick starts for kids!)
    Includes index.
    ISBN 1-885593-57-0 (pbk.)
    1. Clowning—Juvenile literature. 2. Clowns—Juvenile literature. [1. Clowning. 2. Clowns.] I. Title. II. Series.

GV1828 .B87 2001
791.3'3—dc21

2001017370

Quick Starts for Kids!™ series editor: **Susan Williamson**
Interior design: **Linda Williamson, Dawson Design**
Interior illustrations: **Heather Barberie, Rum Raisin Design**
Cover design: **Marie Ferrante-Doyle**
Cover illustrations: **Michael Kline**
Back cover photography of children and page 4: **David A. Seaver**
Printing: **Capital City Press**

Williamson Publishing Co.
P.O. Box 185
Charlotte, VT 05445
(800) 234-8791

Manufactured in the United States of America

10 9 8 7 6 5 4 3 2 1

Dedication

To my kids, Karen, Ronnie, Jon, Eric, and Allyson, who sometimes laugh at my humor.

Also by Ron Burgess
Williamson's *Quick Starts for Kids!*™
YO-YO! Tips & Tricks from a Pro

Clown Jokes and Gags from Silly Willy
<www.members.tripod.com/~sillywillytheclown>

CONTENTS

Is There a Clown Inside You?

Do you like to act silly?
Do you love to make people smile and laugh?
Me too!

Has an adult ever told you that you were a clown?
Has a teacher ever asked you to stop clowning around?
Me too!

People have been calling me a clown all my life, but one day I thought, "Well, if everyone's going to call me a clown, I'd better find out how to be the best one I can be!" So I did.

And with a few supplies and little bit of practice, you can become a clown in real life, just like I did! So grab your best sense of humor and silliness, along with your imagination, and get ready to start clowning around like you've never done before!

Things That Every Clown Should Know

Here are some things to keep in mind as you begin your clowning adventure. You are in for a lot of fun on your way to becoming a world-class clown.

- Your clown face can be perfect for *your* face. No need to make it a copy of someone else's. If you see a clown face that you like, it's OK to borrow from it, but add special touches that say something about *you*.
- Your wig and costume should reflect the type of clown you are. They should be lightweight and comfortable, and your costume should always be loose-fitting for easy movement.
- Your clown name should fit your clown character. It's a good idea not to call yourself "Groucho" when you have a happy face or "Dots" if your costume is stripes or all one color.
- Your props should be exaggerated, whether they're big or small. For example, if you need a comb, try a giant one or a tiny doll comb.
- Remember the clown "don'ts." They really do matter. (See page 54.)
- PRACTICE! Practice everything at least once, and then twice, and then practice it again. In clowning, the smoother the routine, the funnier it is.
- Clowning is like life. It's not a competition. It's meant to be enjoyed!
- Most important: You don't need to act like a clown. You just need to *be a clown!*

I hope you enjoy clowning as much as I do!

Hey, kids,
Learn to be a clown
and take a leap for literacy!

Artful Tricks
&
Teasing Bits

Welcome to the best part of being a clown — clowning around! The more "natural" you act when doing these clown tricks, the funnier they are. Just you wait and see!

These tricks seem so simple that you might think, "Nobody will believe them!" But they do! The sheer simplicity and silliness of them make them work. They can be funny even after the audience finds out it's been fooled. When people ask me to do the tricks again, they laugh all over again!

Teasers & Illusions

Making a Pencil Disappear

The first way to do this trick is to hold a pencil in your right hand. Look to the right. Move your right hand, with the pencil in it, across your body from your left side and out to your right in an underhand throwing motion. Count "1."

Repeat as you count "2."

Then move your right hand back to the same position on your left side. But this time before repeating the throwing motion, place the pencil in your left hand. Continue the throwing motion with your right hand, counting "3." *Look around quizzically for the pencil.*

Quick Starts Tips!™ from a Real Clown

GO FOR THE LAUGH!

When you do a bit like the disappearing pencil, remember that the laugh builds around the final simple part – in this case, looking for the pencil. Here's where your sense of clowning, your timing, and your facial expressions make it fun and funny. No need to rush through. Take your time; your audience will have as much fun with it as you do!

— BE a CLOWN!

The second way is very similar. Hold the pencil in your right hand. Point it down at an object and count "1." Raise your right hand with the pencil toward your head and bring it down. Count "2."

Raise your right hand with the pencil again toward your head, but this time place the pencil behind your ear (or in your wig.)

Bring the empty right hand down and count "3." *Look around for the lost pencil.*

PUSHING A PENCIL THROUGH A GLASS

To make this trick work, hold a glass upside down in one hand. Poke a pencil or pen inside the glass a couple of times so that it clinks against the bottom of the glass being sure to bring the pencil all the way out of the glass each time. On the next time, however, pull the pencil out of the glass and push it upward behind the glass! To the audience, it will look as if the pencil were going right through the glass. This teasing trick is most entertaining if you can hum a goofy song as you do it.

MAKING YOUR LEG DISAPPEAR

Hold a coat or a large scarf (one you can't see through) in front of your body. Lower the coat so the bottom edge touches the floor in front of you. Slip your shoe off one foot. Leave the shoe on the floor and bend your knee up behind the coat. Lift up the coat about 1' (30 cm) off the floor. Suddenly —
hey! — no leg!

CLOWN TACTICS!

When you're trying to convey something through your actions, *slow, clear movements* are the most effective.

1 Take it slowly. Moving quickly is like talking too fast; people won't know what you're trying to say.

2. Exaggerate for emphasis. Exaggeration is like raising your voice when speaking; it attracts attention to the point you want to make, and it helps the audience catch up with you.

WALKING A TIGHTROPE

This trick requires three props: two chairs and a long piece of rope. Walk out to your performing area on the opposite side of the stage, pulling a chair behind you. Make exaggerated motions while you position the chair in just the "right" place with the back of the chair facing center stage. Bring out a second chair and go through the same procedure, lining it up on the other side of the stage. The backs of both chairs should be facing each other, with you in between.

— BE a CLOWN!

Walk off again and come back with the long piece of rope. Tie one end to the top of the back of one chair. As you walk to the other chair, let out the rope. When you get to the second chair, make some quizzical, frustrated looks and gestures as you realize you've run out of rope.

Walk back to the first chair and try it again, hamming it up with more surprised, frustrated looks. Then, pantomime (see page 12) having arrived at a brilliant solution!

Return to the chair and lay it down so the back of the chair is on the ground. Next, take the end of the rope to the other chair. Lay that chair down as well, tying the loose end of the rope to the back. Now you have the rope tied between two chairs, lying on the floor instead of stretched out!

Jump on the rope and carefully "balance" yourself. Walk from one end to the other, almost falling many times! I like to take a BIG bow when I finish. Or, if I'm in a different mood, I'll sometimes curtsy!

BOUNCING A TISSUE

$\mathcal{B}$efore your performance, wrap a tissue around a small rubber ball about the size of a ping-pong ball and put it in your pocket. When you're ready to perform this bit, take the tissue out, making sure you grab the ball with the tissue. Pretend to use the tissue to clean a spot on the floor and then throw the tissue on the floor. It'll bounce right back to your hand!

Pantomime

Clown pantomime involves exaggerated gestures, movements, and expressions to "talk" to an audience without speaking. If I want an audience member to pick up a book and bring it to me, I'll point to the book and gesture to myself. If they don't respond, I'll point again using more emphasis and a stronger gesture pointing to myself. If there's still no response, perhaps I'll shrug my shoulders at the audience to reflect the confusion of the volunteer. I'll make a grouchy face and point a few more times at the book, then gesture wildly to myself. Still no response? I'll lead the volunteer over to the book and point to it until he picks it up. I'll smile and silently applaud. Then, I'll point to myself. When he hands me the book, I'll smile and shake his hand. Then, I'll lead the audience in applause. Whew! It's quite a challenge to communicate without words.

BALANCING A BALLOON ON YOUR NOSE (OR PING-PONG BALL)

The secret to this funny bit happens before the show. Put a small spot of spirit gum on your nose and another on a small balloon. Let both spots dry. At performance time, bend your head back and place the balloon on your nose, making sure the two spots of spirit gum meet and stick. Now move your head back and forth as if you are trying to keep the balloon from falling off, with arms outstretched for emphasis.

Then take a bow and watch your audience laugh as the balloon remains stuck to your nose! (If you want to extend this funny bit, pretend that the balloon is hard to get off. There's all sorts of fun you can have as you pretend to struggle to take it off.)

— BE A CLOWN!

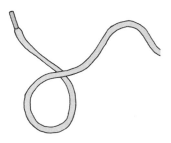

1. LEFT OVER RIGHT

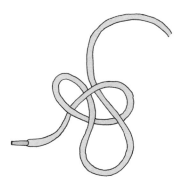

2. BRING LOOP THROUGH

3. PULL THE LOOP WITH YOUR LEFT HAND AND THE ENDS WITH YOUR RIGHT TO TIGHTEN THE KNOT

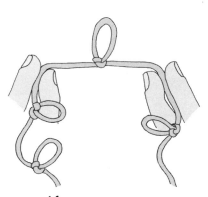

1. MAKE SEVERAL SLIPKNOTS ALONG THE SHOELACE

Silly Willy's Favorite!

Blowing Out Knots

The biggest laughs I get (even from very small children) are from "blowing out" knots. I use a long shoelace and tie a series of slipknots in it. I ask audience members if they know how to take knots out of a shoelace. I tell them that I have a real easy way to take knots out: I just blow on them. Then, I blow on one knot while pulling the shoelace on either side of the knot so the knot comes out.

I squat down in front of a kid and ask her if she would like to try it. I say to her, "When I count to 3, you blow. OK?" Then I begin: "1 – 2 – 2$\frac{1}{2}$ ... Wait, wait! It looks like you're going to blow hard. You're not? Whew! I thought you might blow me right over! OK. We'll start again. 1 – 2 – 3." She blows, and, of course, I fall over, legs in the air, saying with a laugh, "You said *you* weren't going to blow hard!"

Sometimes kids laugh so hard that they can't blow. After I do this with one kid, they all want to try to blow me over. I usually let a couple more kids try, or I have them blow all together as I do a backward somersault. This is *my* favorite trick for getting kids laughing so hard that they cry!

13

Wacky Walkaround & Meet-&-Greet Bits

There are other ways of clowning besides putting on a show. Clowns also perform *walkarounds* and *meet-&-greets*. Walkarounds are short, funny acts that are done for a few people at a party, festival, or picnic. When a clown gets his laugh, he moves on to another group. After touring the whole audience, he starts again with a different gag or trick. Meet-&-greets are handy for greeting people as they enter an event. As each new person enters, a clown can hand them something funny, or do or say something funny, to put them at ease.

Walkarounds are my favorite type of clowning. I love the interaction with people and the different reactions I get using the same material. I also get to do a lot of different things that I don't do in a performance — things like one-on-one bits with audience members. Want examples? Read on!

Quick Starts Jump-Starts™

One-Prop Gags

Is your clown the shy or silent type? Do you have a hard time thinking of what to say to new people? No problem! With these exaggerated prop gags, all you need is a sign and a couple of props.

- Carry a huge pretend razor made out of cardboard and a sign that says "Shave the Whales."
- Carry a tree with gloves hanging from it, along with a sign that reads "California Palm Tree."
- Carry a huge "E" made out of brown paper or cardboard, with a sign that says "Would you like a brownie?" (Get it? A brown "E"!)
- While we're on the subject of letters, carry a box marked "Bee Collection." Then show folks a piece of paper with different sized B's glued on it.
- Carry a branch with plastic eggs attached and a sign that says "Fresh Egg Plant."

— BE A CLOWN!

PRESENTING A FLOWER

For this bit, break off a flower stem right below the flower. Walk around holding both pieces together with your thumb and fingers. Then walk up to someone as you're smelling the flower. Present her with the flower and walk away. As she takes the stem, you walk away with the flower.

Shaking Hands

Clown handshakes always cause a smile, so prepare yourself with these sure-fire giggle-getters!

🖐 When you shake hands with someone smaller than you, pretend that he's really strong; moan and groan and roll your eyes as you fall to your knees.

🖐 When you shake hands, hold on to someone's hand and keep shaking – and shaking – and shaking. "OK, you can stop now," you say as you keep pumping his hand.

🖐 When you shake hands, pretend that the other person is very powerful. Every time your arm goes up, jump up, bouncing up and down with each shake of the hand.

🖐 Pretend that your shaking hands are stuck together. Try to pull yours loose. Be as funny and awkward as you want to be (just remember not to hurt anyone).

ARTFUL TRICKS & TEASING BITS

What Kind of Clown Will You Be?

Growing up, I always enjoyed making people laugh, and I used to love dressing up even when it wasn't Halloween. I invented school projects so I could present them dressed up as a scientist, historical figure, or character from a book. I bought and made silly hats and coats, and wore them to amuse my friends. I practiced for hours in front of a mirror, making different funny faces and expressions. I entered every amateur show I heard about, and I became a professional clown when I was 13. By that time, I'd had plenty of practice and experience, and I knew exactly what kind of clown I wanted to be (but more about that later!).

What kind of clown will you be? Like individuals, clowns come in all sorts, shapes, sizes, colors, and moods. finding your "inner" clown is like getting to know parts of yourself. What do you like most about yourself? What kinds of comments do people make about you? (Do they say things like, "You crack me up!" or "I never know what you're gonna do next!"?) What interests do you enjoy? Do you like to make people laugh out loud, or do you like people to identify with a character?

Finding YOU: Degrees of Comfort

Ask yourself these questions:

1. *What do I do that makes people laugh?*
    Do I tell funny jokes?
    Do I do funny things?
    Do I use funny words?
    What kinds of things do I do that people like?

2. *What kind of personality do I have?*

Am I happy all the time?

Do I laugh at anything?

Do I have a "dry" sense of humor, saying serious things
but in a way that is funny?

Am I a "take-charge" person?

Am I bashful?

Am I outgoing and goofy?

Do I like to make people laugh at me?

Do I like it when people can laugh at themselves?

What makes me laugh?

What makes me feel good?

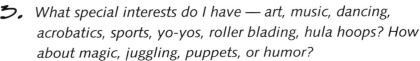

3. *What special interests do I have — art, music, dancing,*
acrobatics, sports, yo-yos, roller blading, hula hoops? How
about magic, juggling, puppets, or humor?

Many clowns are funny by using *slapstick* (physical humor),
pantomime (silent humor), jokes, magic tricks, or talents in juggling,
puppetry, or balancing. Make a list of the interests or talents you
have. Keep them in mind as you develop your clown routine!
(See pages 49–60.) Of course, if your hobby is racing ants or taking naps,
then you might not be clown material, but my guess is that you're a pretty
interesting kid with some interesting hobbies.

> All of this helps you to find and develop your clown character,
> which is very important because this is what you will hang your
> whole clown act on. Your clown face, your clown costume, your
> clown name, your clown bits and actions are all built upon your
> clown character's personality. Now's the time to give all of this a
> lot of thought so you can truly find the clown hiding inside you!

BE A CLOWN!

The Inner Clown

Having trouble finding the clown inside? Make lists of the things you do or say that are funny.

ACTIONS
Funny walks
Tripping over shoelaces
Waving bye-bye with your foot

FUNNY WORDS
sarsaparilla
pickled pigs feet
underwear
rinky dink

JOKES
knock knock jokes
animal riddles
rhyming speech

Do you do or say any of these clowning things? Would you like to?

Match Your "Inner Clown" with Traditional Clowning Styles

So, you think that all clowns are – well – uh – (pause like a good clown) – um – clowns? Well, not so, my friend! There are four types or styles of clowns in the great clowning tradition. The trick is finding what kind of clown best suits the Numero Uno clown – that's YOU! I always knew I was a wild and crazy guy, so naturally I had to be an *Auguste* (aw-GOOST) clown. But for many people, it's a hard decision. Developing your own special clown character takes time. You may go through different types of clown characters, experimenting until you develop a clown character you feel very comfortable with.

THE AUGUSTE CLOWN

The Auguste clown is a happy, silly prankster who likes to play tricks (that often backfire!). (The name comes from a German word that means "clumsy boy.") The Auguste clown is good-natured, clumsy, and forgetful. She's usually the one who doesn't know what's going on, but somehow manages to escape the mess created by her own tricks. Everyone loves the Auguste clown, who mixes things up and gets away with a lot of silliness! Sometimes, the Auguste clown is intentionally funny, and other times she thinks she's doing something correctly when she's really doing it all wrong.

THE AUGUSTE CLOWN

EXAGGERATED FEATURES IN RED AND BLACK

MISMATCHED COSTUME OF BRIGHT, CLASHING STRIPES, POLKA DOTS, AND PLAIDS

CLOTHES EITHER TOO LARGE, TOO SMALL, OR BOTH

Picture This!

Picture a big, wrapped box on a stage. What would the Auguste clown do? He would probably walk across the stage and trip over it. Or he might try to kick it or pick it up and shake it to find out what's inside. He might even play catch with it or shrug his shoulders and throw up his hands in an "I don't know" gesture to the audience. Then, perhaps, he'd leave the box and begin another funny bit.

THE WHITEFACE CLOWN

The two most popular types of Whiteface clown are the *Classic Whiteface* clown and the *Comedy Whiteface* clown.

BE A CLOWN!

THE CLASSIC WHITEFACE CLOWN

This clown is silky smooth — and in more ways than one! Shrewd and sophisticated are good words to describe the Classic Whiteface clown, a very "take-charge" type of clown. This is the clown that gets others into trouble and blames others when things go wrong!

Now, you might be thinking, "So what's funny about a character like this?" Well, the Classic Whiteface clown plays on our tendency to laugh at show-offs or know-it-alls. These clowns think they're better than everyone else, but we know better! We can laugh at these prim and proper characters.

The Classic Whiteface costume is smooth, too — stylish and elegant. It is often made of satin, silk, or other dressy materials, and decorated with sequins, rhinestones, pompoms, sparkles, ruffles, beads, ribbons, and bows.

ALL-WHITE MAKEUP BASE COVERING FACE, NECK, AND EARS

POSSIBLY A SMALL DETAIL (SUCH AS HEART OR TEAR) ON FACE

SMALL AMOUNTS OF RED AND BLACK FOR FACIAL FEATURES

SOMETIMES GLITTER AS HIGHLIGHT

ELEGANT, MATCHING COSTUME

THE CLASSIC WHITEFACE CLOWN

ALL-WHITE MAKEUP BASE COVERING FACE, NECK, AND EARS

COSTUME TENDS TO MATCH

EXAGGERATED FEATURES IN RED AND BLACK

THE COMEDY WHITEFACE CLOWN

THE COMEDY WHITEFACE CLOWN

The Comedy Whiteface clown is like the Auguste clown — a real joker with tricks up her sleeve — except with whiteface makeup all over! When a Comedy Whiteface clown performs, you might see him acting like a Classic Whiteface, or an Auguste, or a combination of the two! In other words, *anything goes* with the Comedy Whiteface clown!

The Comedy Whiteface costume, too, is pretty much a free-for-all — elegant, comical, or a combination of both — but colors are more likely to match in a Comedy Whiteface outfit than they might in an Auguste costume.

WHAT KIND OF CLOWN WILL YOU BE?

Picture This!

Picture another big, wrapped box on a stage. A Classic Whiteface clown might walk out with his hands behind his back, his nose in the air as if he owned the world. He doesn't stop at the box (after all, why would such an important clown be impressed with one silly box?), but then his curiosity causes him to sneak a peek when he thinks no one is looking. Next, he pushes it slightly with his foot a few times. He picks it up, or smells it, or shakes it. He might put it down, sniff snobbishly, and walk off. Or he might tell another clown to carry "his" package back to his house.

Picture This!

There's that box again on stage. The Comedy Whiteface might skip happily by it. She stops suddenly, makes exaggerated surprised faces, and then turns and looks at the box and then at the audience a few times. She might walk around the box and touch it quickly, push it with her finger, or sit on it while looking all around. She might rip a small piece of the wrapping paper and then check to see if anyone had seen her. She continues ripping until she is in a frenzy of paper flying off the box. Then she gleefully marches off with the box, leaving the paper behind.

BE A CLOWN!

THE CHARACTER CLOWN

The character clown is like a clown cartoon. She can depict a *storybook character* (such as Mother Goose), a *person* such as a movie star or the president, or an *occupation* (perhaps a cowboy, a policeman, a ballplayer, a nurse, a firefighter, or a scientist). While the costume should identify the character being portrayed, makeup can be Auguste, Classic Whiteface, or Comedy Whiteface.

Picture This!

How would a character clown react to that box on stage? That would depend on the character. A cowboy clown might lasso it and pull it off stage. A policeman might walk around it, inspecting it while swinging his nightstick. Then, he might put his foot on it and write it a ticket. A scientist might pull out a magnifying glass and examine every inch of the box. A princess might sit by the box and dream up a wonderful story.

Quick Starts Tips!™ from a Real Clown

QUICK CLOWN CHECKLIST

Auguste: Silly, goofy, always fooling around. We laugh *with* him and *at* him.

Classic Whiteface: Pompous, prim, and proper. We laugh *at* him.

Comedy Whiteface: Could behave like an Auguste or Classic Whiteface, or combination. We laugh *with* her.

Character: Always dressed like some character, but could behave like any of the above.

WHAT KIND OF CLOWN WILL YOU BE?

The Name Game

There are many different things that can influence your choice of the perfect clown name. It could be your clown's personality. It could be the costume that you wear. It could be something that you say, or do, or like. Or it just might be a name that you've always liked.

Sometimes, you begin with one name and then when your character comes together – with type of clown, costume, face, and personality – your clown name doesn't quite fit you anymore. No matter. Change your name until *all the pieces* fit together!

Want to know how I chose my clown name? My original name was "Uncle Ron," but that seemed too formal. Then I picked "Rainbow" because my costume has all the colors of the rainbow. That name worked for a while – that is, until I remembered something my mother often said to me when I was very young: "Ronald stop acting like a Silly Willy." Ah-ha! The perfect clown name for me! I've been Silly Willy ever since.

What's in a Name?

Are you a Noun Clown, a Verb Blurb, or a Rhyme Mime (now, *there's* a challenge!)? Here's a list of some name categories that might get you in the Name Game mood. Try combos, along with made-up words and sounds that make you smile. Just remember: The first clown name that you pick, like your clown makeup and costume, doesn't have to be your final choice. Try on different names just like you try on costumes.

Take a look at the clowns illustrated here. See if you can think of names for them based on what you see. Then compare your names to the ones I made up (at the bottom of the page). Remember, mine aren't necessarily the "right" ones. Yours may be better!

— BE A CLOWN!

Action Verbs

Are you an on-the-move clown? These clowns attract attention by the things they do. What kind of names do they make you think of?

Clothing Details

Does a single feature define you? These clowns get a kick from their costumes!

Assorted Other Clownful Names

These are the kinds of names that you may think of simply because you like the sound of them or the things they make you think of.

Food

Name your favorite one. Who knows? You might even be able to work it into your act!

Names Associated with Sounds (or No Sounds!)

So you play a musical instrument that you'd like to incorporate into your act? Or are you the silent type? Either way, there's plenty of room for creativity!

Personal Traits

Sad Tad, Happy Cappy ... or Silly Willy! A picture's worth a thousand words!

RON'S NAMES: *Action Verbs:* Bubbles; *Clothing:* Patches; *Clownful Names:* Blossoms; *Food:* Popcorn; *Sounds:* Bongo; *Traits:* Sadsack.

WHAT KIND OF CLOWN WILL YOU BE?

Funny Faces

My clown face evolved over a few years. I started with a Halloween makeup kit, a sponge nose, and a rubber bald head from a costume shop. At first I had everything BIG — big, white eyes and a big, wide, white mouth. Later, I added a black outline around the eyes and mouth because it was hard to apply the white makeup evenly.

When I looked at pictures of myself in my clown outfit, my eyes looked lost with all the white makeup around them, so I learned how to apply makeup to make my eyes stand out. Then, I noticed that most other clowns colored their lips black instead of having only a wide, white muzzle (the area under the nose to the chin and cheek to cheek), so I made my lips black instead of red.

I also noticed that other clowns had red cheeks and chins, so I began to do my cheeks in red, upside down teardrops with a drop of white in each center that looked like a reflection of light. And eventually I changed my nose from a large, 2" (5 cm) sponge ball to a small, round plastic nose less than 1" (2.5 cm) round. Finally, I changed my wig — first from a rubber bald head to a multicolored Halloween wig, and then from the Halloween wig to a real wig I could cut and style.

Lately, I've removed the makeup from below my nose to my upper lip. That way, when I have to sneeze, my makeup won't run! I also outline my complete face in black because I think it pulls all the makeup together.

You're One of a Kind!

 One of the most important clowning decisions you'll make is about your face! Just imagine – you can design your own one-of-a-kind clown face! What you're after is a clown face that expresses who your inner clown is. And be very sure it's a face you're comfortable in! It takes time to develop a face that reflects your clown personality, so feel free to experiment with different ideas.

THE FIRST STEP IS EASY. Look in a mirror. Your clown face is looking right at you! No one in the world looks quite like you do. See for yourself! Look at all of the lines, creases, and shapes you can make with that good-looking mug in the mirror. Look at your special features – your eyes, nose, mouth, forehead, and ears. Does your mouth turn up at the corners? Do you have freckles that give you a happy look? Do your eyes smile, or are they sleepy eyes? You can use all of these characteristics to create a clown face that's completely you! But before you start painting it on, it's a good idea to design your face on paper so you know how and where you want the face paint to go!

CLOWN FACE CALISTHENICS

 Don't leave the mirror yet. It's time to give your face a workout (while the rest of you observes!).

> *Stick out* your tongue.
> *Cross* your eyes.
> *Wiggle* your nose.
> *Show* your teeth.
> *Puff up* your cheeks.

What do you see when you do all these things?
Do you see any natural lines to follow with makeup?
What parts of your face move?

BE A CLOWN!

Poke your tongue into your cheek and move it around, first on one side of your mouth and then on the other. *Poke* your tongue under your lips and roll it around top and bottom.

How does it look?

Would it look funnier with makeup on?

Make silly faces: smile, frown, squint, pout, cry, grin, look mad, and look happy.

      Do all of these things with your mouth closed tightly.

      Do them with your mouth wide open.

How do the lines and creases on your face move when you do all of these things?

Can these be emphasized with makeup?

 What shape is your face?

    Is it round, square, or triangular?

      Is it long or short?

        Wide or thin?

What about your features — eyes, nose, and mouth?

Are they big, little, round, oval?

Do they move when you make faces?

How can you emphasize them?

EXAGGERATE!

Does everyone know you for your wonderful smile? Your cool hair? For fun, draw a self-portrait, exaggerating certain features, perhaps making your freckles enormous or your smile go from ear to ear. These exaggerated drawings, called *caricatures*, are often used in political cartoons in newspapers, and they are great practice for finding your clown face, too.

Not an Artist?

It may sound easy to draw a simple outline of your face, but what if you don't think of yourself as an artist? No problem! Just trace. Find a picture in a magazine, preferably a full-page face looking forward (often used in makeup ads). It doesn't have to look exactly like you. You just need a face with the same basic shape as your face.

The second step is to start drawing sketches of possible clown faces. Trace the face outline, making several copies. Then, on each copy, mix and match the different noses, mouths, eyebrows, and cheeks from those shown here. Better yet, take into account your facial features and sketch your own face (think in terms of shapes — circles, ovals, triangles — to make it easier).

BE A CLOWN!

Another good way to plan your face is to use a computer. Scan in a close-up photograph of yourself and use a basic paint program to try different faces.

FINISHING TOUCHES ⊙

ROUNDING OUT YOUR DESIGN ON PAPER

You can enhance your clown expressions by taking full advantage of your features. Start with the nose: Are you going to paint yours or wear a bulbous red one? Would you like a little, thin one or a great big, round one?

Eyebrows can also add to your permanent expression. They can make you look happy, surprised, or mad (though, as a clown, you'll probably want to stay away from angry faces). Most clowns draw on eyebrows on their foreheads above their own eyebrows. This "opens up" the face for better visibility by the audience, makes the face more "cartoonish," and projects expressions over a distance. Just remember to consider the size and shape of your forehead and the placement of your wig when you're thinking about how and where to place your eyebrows.

Color Me Magnifico!

Nothing like a little color to bring your character to life! Clowns generally use only three colors – white, red, and black (and sometimes a little blue for highlights such as teardrops). Why such a limited palette? Well, light green and yellow tend to make your face look sickly! And dark greens, blues, and purples turn your face into a monster face – not very clownish. Stay away from red makeup on your eyelids because it makes your eyes look bloodshot. More important, though, the dye could irritate your eyes.

SUPPLIES

Clown makeup supplies can be purchased at theatrical supply houses, cosmetic suppliers, party stores, or clown and magician shops. To be completely prepared, you'll probably want your first makeup kit to include:

- White *water-based* face paint or "pancake" makeup

- Red, black, and light blue *water-based* face paints or grease pencils

- Paintbrushes. When using water-based face paints (which I highly recommend), you'll want a small brush for each color and a large brush or a soft, smooth facial sponge for white.

- Baby shampoo, baby oil, or makeup remover to remove makeup

- Facecloths, towels, napkins, cotton swabs, or facial tissues to remove makeup

- Theatrical or facial glitter (Never use art and craft glitter on your face. Never put any kind of glitter near your eyes.)

- An *old* shirt to wear while you apply makeup to keep it off your costume

Paint It On!

Follow the following easy steps to apply a terrific Auguste face or Whiteface.

Paint Pointers

Though professional clowns use grease paint to create their clown faces, I strongly suggest that *you use only water-based face paint.* Face paints are easily available from craft, costume, and toy stores and they're much easier to work with. Grease paints are harder to find (they're limited to theatrical or clown supply stores), and they're much more difficult to apply. Keep it easy – go with face paints!

Also, when professional clowns apply makeup, they cover all of the exposed areas of the head, including the front and back of the ears and neck! I'm going to describe how to put on just the face. It still looks great and is much simpler (and much less messy) to get off.

BE A CLOWN!

Protecting That Fabulous Face!

Never apply anything but face paint or theatrical makeup to your face. Anything else — such as paint, markers, shoe polish, white out, or dye — can be very harmful to your skin.

APPLYING YOUR MAKEUP: AUGUSTE AND WHITEFACE

✫ Always start with a clean, dry face. (Great advice anytime!)

✫ Always apply makeup from top to bottom, starting at the forehead and working down to the chin. As you work down, close one eye at a time to do each eyelid.

✫ Apply a smooth even coat, filling in all the creases and lines on your face. (Of course, at your age, there won't be many creases, if any. At my age, they're as deep as the Grand Canyon!)

✫ Don't apply one thick coat of makeup because heavy makeup flakes off. Instead, wait until the first coat dries and then apply a second or third coat, if needed, for full coverage.

✫ If your face design has one color outlined with another color, apply the base color first; then apply the outline. For example, if your lower lip is colored red and outlined with black, apply the red first, then outline with black.

✫ Apply colors going from the lightest to darkest, with the lightest color going on first and the darkest color going on last. Apply white, for example, before the red, and the red followed by the black. Be careful not to smear the colors.

✫ Don't apply any color but white to the area between your nose and your upper lip. The contrast between the white above your upper lip and the red or black of your lower lip will help to add more expression to your face.

AUGUSTE STYLE

WHITE FACE PAINT JUST FOR ACCENTS
EXAGGERATED FEATURES
RED FACE PAINT
BLACK FACE PAINT

WHITEFACE STYLE

ALL-WHITE MAKEUP COVERS WHOLE FACE
RED FACE PAINT
BLACK FACE PAINT
HEART OR TEAR DETAIL (OPTIONAL)
FACIAL GLITTER (OPTIONAL) TO
HIGHLIGHT

What's the Diff?

AUGUSTE STYLE

1. Apply white paint only to the features you want to accentuate (nose, eyebrows, mouth, cheeks, etc.).

2. Exaggerate facial features with red and black.

WHITEFACE STYLE

1. White paint covers your *entire face*, spreading it as evenly as possible.

2. After your whiteface makeup has dried completely, add the other colors, on top of the white makeup base. For the *Classic* Whiteface, use small amounts of red and black for the facial features, with a tear or heart as a highlight. For the *Comedy* Whiteface, use more red and black paint to exaggerate the features.

3. Apply facial glitter (optional) last.

BE A CLOWN!

Take It Off!

Bravo! Your performance was a smash hit! Now it's time to retire your clown face for the evening. The best way to remove your clown makeup is by using baby shampoo, baby oil, cooking oil, or makeup remover.

1. Place a small amount on your fingertips or on a warm damp cloth, and lightly massage your face, ears, neck – wherever you have makeup.
2. Let it sit for a few seconds; then wipe it off with a washcloth or facial tissue. Repeat, if necessary, and rinse thoroughly.
3. Treat yourself to some moisturizer. It will make your face feel fresh and ready for the next performance!

Comical Costumes

As important as your clown face is in determining your character, so is your clown costume! Don't be shy about trying out all sorts of possibilities as you look for an outfit to suit your clown's style because, like your clown face, your clown costume will be with you year in and year out. The goal is for your costume to work for you and *with* you. There are just two hard and fast rules where costumes are concerned:

☆ Your clown face and costume should be a perfect match to help bring out your true clown character! You want to send a clear message to your audience about who you are.

☆ While you're putting together a costume that's comical, don't forget to make it comfortable, too! That means not making your clothing uncomfortably tight or loose, or having dragging parts that might get in the way of your clown act.

Put it all together, and you have "Silly Willy," the Auguste!

white face paint for accents

exaggerated features in red and black

(note the lack of makeup between my nose and upper lip)

wacky accessories

mismatched costume of bright, clashing striipes and checks

oversized shoes

Dress Your Auguste & Comedy Whiteface Clown

Want to have some super fun? Show up at a breakfast dressed in glorious unstyle! The fashion police won't know whether to laugh or cry! Costumes for the Auguste and Comedy Whiteface clowns are a fashion designer's nightmare, but a dream come true for a clown like you! Their clothes mix and mismatch big plaids, big stripes, big checks, and big polka dot patterns. The Auguste costume mismatches colors as well, while colors in the Comedy Whiteface costume tend to match and flow. The bolder and brighter, the better, with eye-popping primary colors! Experiment with colors and patterns to see how much fun your costume can be!

Quick Starts Jump-Starts™

Where to Start?

Be careful what you wish for: Having no rules sometimes makes choosing more difficult! How about beginning at a local thrift shop or yard sale, where clothing is not only plentiful, but inexpensive as well? Or perhaps an adult in your home has some old, oversized clothing that's no longer needed. Better not "borrow" anything, though. Clown clothes take a beating from makeup, tricks, or even trimming, so only use clothes that are given to you "for keeps."

BE A CLOWN!

A WILD & WACKY SHIRT!

My first clown shirt was from the plus-size shirts in the women's department at a local store. It was a white jersey with big, red polka dots. I sewed on mismatched, colored cuffs and a big collar cut from a thrift store shirt. Today, I wear good-quality polo shirts in loud colors with striped patterns. (One teenager saw my outfit and wondered how she could copy it for school. Pretty soon, clowns will have to wear regular clothes to be funny!)

BEFORE

☆ Look for shirts with multicolored stripes, large polka dots, or loud colors with short sleeves, long sleeves, or sleeves cut off at the elbow.

☆ Use fabric paint to decorate a brightly colored T-shirt or sweatshirt.

☆ In thrift shops, look for brightly colored jackets or vests. Sew on large buttons or glue on colorful strips and patches.

☆ Add neon polka dots using glow-in-the-dark joggers' tape.

AFTER

Quick Starts Tips!™ from a Real Clown

NO LOGOS!

Stay away from T-shirts or sweatshirts with writing or cartoon characters on them. They're funny once, but then the audience gets bored with them.

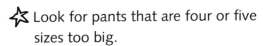

PANTS & PANTALOONS!

I made my first clown pants from pajama bottoms because pajamas tend to be baggy, which is perfect for a clown. They also come in loud colors and prints. Just cut off the legs below the knees, take out the elastic waistband and — instant clown pants!

★ Look for pants that are four or five sizes too big.

★ Sew plenty of pockets inside the waistband to hold all of your clown props.

★ Hold the trousers up with crazy, clown-colored suspenders, or a rope or scarf tied around your waist.

★ Cut the pants' legs off at the knee or roll them up to show off your beautiful striped or mismatched socks.

★ Glue or sew on colorful strips and patches to liven up dull-colored pants.

ACCENTUATE WITH ACCESSORIES!

◎ Make or buy an extra-large bow tie or an extra-wide, extra-long necktie that hangs between your knees. Attach the tie to your neck with an elastic band so it will snap back in place when you stretch it out. (If you're going to wear a tie, you don't always need a collar on your shirt since ties look even funnier on a bare neck.)

◎ Go the other way and have a teeny, tiny necktie or bow tie.

◎ Make huge paper flowers.

◎ Socks can be stripes, polka dots, or checks in any loud color you can find. The crazier and wilder, the better!

— BE a CLOWN!

Hats can be derbies, high hats, berets, caps, hats with ear flaps, or men's soft hats. Try tiny, doll-size hats held on with bobby pins, or extra-large hats that come down over your ears. Try hats in bright colors or plaids, checks, stripes, or polka dots. Stay away from baseball caps though, or you'll soon learn what other clowns know: Baseball caps aren't very funny.

COMICAL COSTUMES

A Method to the Madness!

Accessories can add to the fun – or they can define a character. Think about all of the ways your costume and act can pull together to illustrate your clown persona.

❀ Are you going to be a clown who always carries a tiny umbrella and does a lot of jokes based on that prop?

❀ Are you a clown who is always looking for your purse – either an enormous one or a teeny, tiny one – and finding just what you need inside?

❀ Are snapping suspenders part of your gag?

❀ Is a big heart part of who you are – and does your costume have one bulging out of your shirt?

MAKING YOUR SHOES

My first clown shoes were the largest white tennis shoes I could find. I painted them with fabric paint in bright colors, with different patterns on each shoe. I stuffed the toes with tissue (you can use newspaper or cloth, too), and I put a pair of slippers inside them to make them comfortable (I told you they were large!). I bought different-colored neon shoelaces, and when someone noticed that I had two different shoes on, I told him I had a pair just like them at home!

Auguste and Comedy Whiteface clown shoes are always oversized. (Look for them in big boxes in dollar stores or discount stores.) Buy a pair of extra-large white tennis shoes that you can walk in while already wearing a pair of your shoes or slippers. Then, just do what I did, starting with padding the toes.

What if tennis shoes don't seem to fit your clown personality? Would big, furry animal slippers be better? How about flippers? You can wear them as is, or paint and decorate them with dots, stars, and different-colored shapes. For every clown, there's a different idea!

BE A CLOWN!

WIGGING OUT!

Wigs can be bought at party stores, joke shops, or clown and magician shops. But why buy when you can make a one-of-a-kind wig to suit your unique clown character?

✳ Wear a clean, white string mop, leaving it as is for white hair, or trim it and dye it any bright color.

✳ Make a wig from a hat and some yarn. Cut a piece of cloth 1" (2.5 cm) wide and long enough to fit inside your hatband. Cut pieces of yarn about 6" (15 cm) long. Glue the pieces of yarn to the strip and then glue the strip inside the hat.

✳ Cut strips of construction paper 1" (2.5 cm) wide. Curl them by rolling them around a pencil. Then, glue them around the inside of a hat so they hang down.

✳ Take a gallon-sized freezer bag; use glue to attach packing peanuts or shredded paper to one half. Let dry. Then, repeat on the other half and wear as a wig. (Of course, never put a plastic bag over your face!)

Quick Starts Tips!™ from a Real Clown

WATCH OUT!

Big shoes can mean big falls — not necessarily for laughs, either. Practice walking in your shoes, and if you find yourself tripping, then skip (no pun intended) the really big shoes. There are plenty of other ways to make your costume fun!

Costume Your Classic Whiteface Clown

Do you prefer the elegant touch? The Classic Whiteface clown's costume is a stylish and well-fitting one- or two-piece jumper outfit. The costume is usually color-coordinated in two or three bright colors, but if those don't suit your clown's personality, try softer pastel colors.

GOING "GLAM"!

Get ready to have fun putting together your Classic Whiteface costume because there's a lot to choose from!

• At thrift shops and yard sales, look for satin or flashy one- or two-piece pajama sets. Silk- and satin-type blouses with puffy sleeves and coordinated matching pants make a great Classic Whiteface costume!

• Try a well-fitting, one-piece, long-sleeved coverall set. Dye it or paint it with fabric paints in pastel or bright, vibrant colors. (You can also color one side a bright color and the opposite side a matching or coordinating color.)

• Sleeves and pant legs can be wide and bell-shaped, or they can be gathered at the wrists and ankles by tying them with colorful scarves from thrift shops or tag sales.

• Glue on glitter, sequins, rhinestones, sparkles, beads, pom-poms, ruffles, lace, ribbons, or bows. But don't go overboard. Remember that you're outfitting an elegant clown.

• Shoes usually fit normally. Try slippers or ballet shoes that are color-coordinated with your costume. Decorate them with the materials you used on your costume. Try adding bells, large pom-poms, or bows to the toes.

• Use tight-fitting gloves and stockings or kneesocks in white or a color that matches your costume.

a clown!

- For extra flair, cover your neck with a ruff or pleated collar made of lace, cloth, or crepe paper gathered around your neck. Start with a piece of cloth you like that measures about 10" (25 cm) x 36" (90 cm). Sew running stitches down one of the long sides, gathering the fabric as you sew. Now it's ready to wear; just tie off the ruff at the back of the neck!

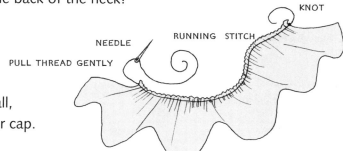

- Top off your outfit with a small, pointed hat or a short, flat hat or cap.

MAKING A CLASSIC WHITEFACE TOPPER

Find a large sheet of poster board. Measure your head where you want the hat to fit. Roll the poster board into a cone shape until the big end is the size of your head. Tape the cone to hold it together. Cut off the bottom triangles so the hat has an even, round shape. Now decorate the cone with ribbons, pom-poms, glitter, or anything else you like.

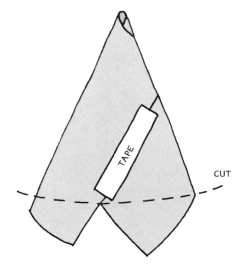

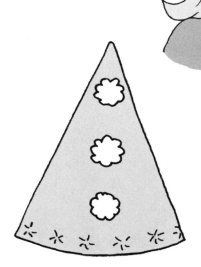

DON'T CUT THE EDGE

HOW TO LOOK BALD!

A Classic Whiteface clown usually has no hair, so buy a white skullcap at a costume shop or make one. Fit the top of a pair of white cotton tights onto your head, tuck your hair inside, and cut off the extra after you've made a knot at the top. You can cover your ears; or if you want them to show, cut holes for them. Then, apply white makeup.

THE WELL APPOINTED, UNDERSTATED MALE CLASSIC WHITEFACE

Boys might prefer a more simple Classic Whiteface costume like the one worn by the famous movie star Gene Kelly in the movie *An American in Paris*:

- ☺ a large, white, collarless shirt that hangs to just above the knees
- ☺ white, wide-leg pants
- ☺ three or four red or black pom-poms or buttons sewn down the front of the shirt
- ☺ white gloves and tennis shoes, or black or red gloves and shoes to match the buttons
  An oversized tuxedo or tuxedo vest and pants are also fun.

46

BE a CLOWN!

Outfit Your Character Clown

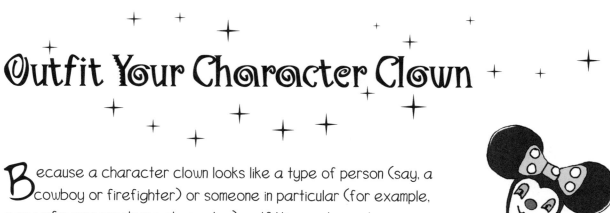

Because a character clown looks like a type of person (say, a cowboy or firefighter) or someone in particular (for example, a specific nursery rhyme character), outfitting a character clown is a bit like dressing up for Halloween. The biggest difference is the face, because a character clown still has to have that special touch — either Auguste, Classic Whiteface, or Comedy Whiteface makeup! So start collecting the items you need to outfit your character and see if your family members or friends can tell who your character is!

COMICAL COSTUMES

make It match:
Personality, Clown Face, & Costume

You sure do know a lot about clown types and styles so far. Here's a fun way to pull it all together. Match the characteristics listed below with the appropriate clown styles you've learned about. Some answers may be true of more than one type of clown. (Gotcha!)

Auguste clown
Classic Whiteface clown
Comedy Whiteface clown
Character clown

1. fancy satin costumes
2. can have elegant or comical costume with colors that are likely to match
3. a clown version of a particular occupation, person, or figure in a story
4. a white face with exaggerated features in black and white
5. good-natured, silly, and clumsy
6. usually bald
7. shoes that are oversized and goofy
8. a real trickster with a white face
9. wildly mismatched, oversized clothes in bright, mismatched colors
10. a white face with small amounts of red and black highlights
11. can have either kind of face – Auguste or Whiteface
12. the "take-charge" clown
13. exaggerated black and red highlights
14. shoes that are small and well-fitting
15. Silly Willy

Silly Sight-&-Sound Gags!

With the right timing and emphasis, you can make scratching your head, swatting an imaginary fly, or trying to get comfy on a park bench funny — hilariously funny. What really brings out the laughter is the clown OVER-reaction at the end of each bit. This is best conveyed by making big, sweeping motions and expressions.

Of course, your best performance is going to happen when you feel confident. And a big part of that feeling comes from being comfortable in your character. Take a look at the many funny bits described here. Which ones do you think fit your clown personality? No need to use them all. Find the ones that feel right for your character. Test them out to find the ones that you enjoy doing and know you can do well; then fine-tune them and put them together for your own terrific clown routine!

Make a Funny Entrance

"CLIMBING" INTO VIEW

What better way is there to make a good first impression than to start your act off with a laugh? Stand behind a doorway so that your audience cannot see you. Pretend that the doorway is actually a wall laying on its side, with the long edge of the doorway the top of the "wall."

"Climb" up the wall (in other words, through the doorway) by moving one hand around the edge of the doorway to try to get a hold. Then move the other hand up and try to hold on. With lots of groaning, and huffing, and puffing, pull your head into view.

With your head and hands now sideways in the doorway, look around and smile dumbly. Then, say, "Uh-oh," as you slowly start to "slide" down the wall. Struggle to pull yourself up again, and then pull yourself "over the wall" (through the door).

x

BE A CLOWN!

Do the Moonwalk

You'll never find a smoother entrance than this one! The walk got its name because you'll look as if you're defying gravity — skimming above the ground, moving in a very cool way!

To start, bend your right knee and lift your right foot from the arch, sliding the foot backward. The left foot is raised as the right one seems to "land" in back of you. Actually, you adjust its position so that it's just under you. The second your right heel hits the ground, begin lifting the left foot, and vice versa, so both legs are always in a state of changing position. You'll appear to be slide-walking backward!

The secret is to make super-smooth movements as you work both legs simultaneously. Hold your arms and head as if they were floating out from you. You don't travel very far in this dance, but it's a great optical illusion.

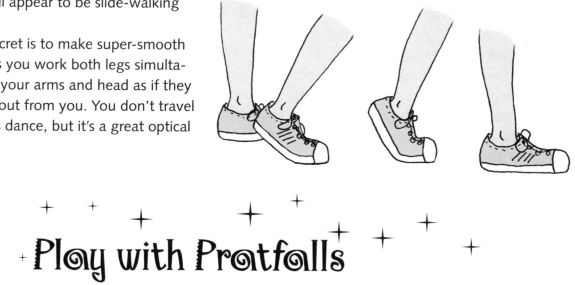

Play with Pratfalls

Clowning would be pretty painful if clowns got hurt as often as they pretend to! Tripping, walking into walls, and falling down — that's what clowns appear to do, but they don't *really*. They just make it look that way. It's all part of the act.

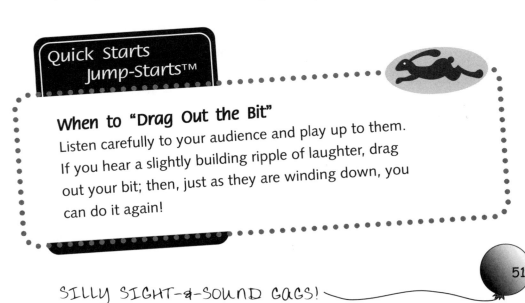

Quick Starts Jump-Starts™

When to "Drag Out the Bit"
Listen carefully to your audience and play up to them. If you hear a slightly building ripple of laughter, drag out your bit; then, just as they are winding down, you can do it again!

SILLY SIGHT-&-SOUND GAGS!

WALKING INTO A WALL OR DOOR

What kind of a book teaches kids how to walk into walls? A book on clowning! The first way to carry off this funny bit is to walk up to a wall quickly, looking the other way. When you're very close to the wall, kick it and raise your hand to hold your head at the same time. If you're a Comedy Whiteface clown or an Auguste clown, like I am, then you'll want to make a loud painful noise and stagger with your eyes rolling around in your head! Oh, my achin' noggin! The Classic Whiteface clown, on the other hand, will compose himself in a very snobbish manner, pretending that it didn't happen.

The second way is to walk up to the wall, looking the other way. Just before you hit the wall with your body or head, pull one hand up and smack the wall. In the same motion, quickly bring your hands up to hold the injured spot while you moan and groan your way to laughs.

TRIPPING

Being a clown, you *always* trip over things. (You might even trip over things that aren't really there!) Tripping is almost like skipping. To trip the way professional clowns do, step off on one foot and then bring the second foot up behind the first foot so that it touches the heel of the first foot. Just as your second foot touches the heel of your first foot, lean forward a little bit, making a little hop with your first foot.

You might want to make a sound when you "trip," such as saying, "Oops!" or blowing a horn if you have one. And don't forget the quizzical look back at the "thing" you tripped over! To get more laughs (and applause), exaggerate your going back to "examine" the spot where you tripped. To top it off, you could wipe up the spot with a hankie.

— BE a CLOWN!

FALLING DOWN

Clowns call this a *pratfall*, and it requires some careful practice so you don't hurt yourself. Do all of your practicing on a rug with pillows on the floor, making sure there is nothing around (such as a table, chair, or if outside, a fence or rocks) to get hurt on.

To Fall Forward

Hold both of your hands about 1' (30 cm) in front of your chest, shoulder high. Keep your body perfectly straight, without bending your knees. Fall forward and catch yourself on your hands (as though you're beginning to do a push-up). Practice this a few times until you get a feel for it. Then, try falling forward with your hands by your side. Halfway down, pull your hands up into position (1'/30 cm from your shoulders) and catch yourself.
If you do it quickly, it will look as if you fell straight down. Moan, groan, roll around, and ham it up!

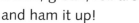

To Fall Backward

Squat down quickly and put one or two hands behind you to catch yourself. Lower yourself onto your bottom. Then, straighten out your legs, roll onto your back, and kick up your feet.

SILLY SIGHT-&-SOUND GAGS!

THE FIVE CLOWN "DON'TS"

1 Don't hurt people's feelings.
"Jokes" that embarrass, insult, or make fun of people are no fun for anyone. No exceptions. A real clown sticks to jokes that make *everyone* feel good.

2 Don't physically hurt anyone.
Hitting someone is not funny. Cartoon characters hit and smash and bang, but in real life those things hurt, so don't hit yourself or anyone else with anything. Even if you are pretending, someone may hit you back for real.

3 Don't throw things.
You might hurt someone or break something when you throw an object, and someone might hurt you when throwing it back to you.

4 Don't spray or throw water.
Watching cartoons, movies, or TV shows, you may see a clown squirting water at a person. That's only make-believe. Professional clowns don't do that because they know that people don't like to have real tricks played on them.

5 Don't be annoying.
Clowns know when to be funny — and when not to. Don't run around telling people how funny you are, or irritating them with silly gadgets and noises. If you annoy people, they won't think you're funny.

Keep the humor where the spotlight is: on YOU!

BE A CLOWN!

Sly Sound Effects

SQUEAKING BODY PARTS

Put one finger in your ear and move it around. As you do, the audience hears it squeak! Rub your nose or your eye, and hear it squeak! You can create this wacky sound effect by holding a squeaker in your pocket with the opposite hand. Squeak it as you move your finger. (You can find squeakers at magic shops, trick stores, and some gift shops.)

• •

CATCHING A BALL IN A BAG

This sounds like a real easy trick if you have a ball, but what if you don't have one? That's what makes this bit funny! All you need is a paper bag (lunch bags are a good size). Reach into the bag, pretending to take a ball out. Pretend to bounce the imaginary ball and catch it. Throw it up in the air and catch it after it bounces on the floor. (Don't forget those exaggerated movements as your head and eyes follow the imaginary ball.) "Throw" the ball up in the air and reach out with the bag. As you catch the pretend ball, everyone hears "plop" as you pretend that it's fallen into the bag. Do it a second time. There's that plop again. "Throw" the pretend ball to someone and have her toss it up in the air for you to catch. Plop — in the bag once more.

"How'd he do that?" your audience wonders! The secret to this trick is the way you hold the bag. With your third finger and thumb, hold the bag on the side closest to you (the side the audience can't see). To make the noise as the ball falls into the bag, snap your thumb and third finger with the bag in between. Try it with a sheet of paper; it's fun! Make sure you follow the invisible ball with your eyes and exaggerate with slowed movements, because this really improves this trick. If you happen to miss the snap once in a while, pretend that you missed the ball. Then, you can pretend to pick it up from the floor and try again!

Entertain the Eyes!

GETTING ALL STUCK UP

"Accidentally" tearing or breaking a prop on stage (say, for example, that bag you used to catch the ball on page 55) can start a whole new gag routine with masking tape. "All I need is a small piece of tape to fix this," you can tell your audience as you rip off 6' (180 cm) of tape. Your funny bit has begun as the tape gets tangled up in a big ball!

Once you have a tangled-up ball of tape, stick it under your arm and try another piece. This time, as you tape the broken or torn object, tape your other hand to it. Drop the tape and pick it up in back of your leg so it gets stuck to your body or hat or anything else that's in the way! Then, since you can't rip it off, try to tear it with your teeth so it gets stuck to your mouth! Pull it off so it gets stuck to your hand. Stick it under your foot so it gets stuck to your shoe (does this mean your shoe gets stuck to the floor?). Take the tape off your shoe and then discover that you can't shake it loose from your hand. Pull it with the other hand so that it sticks there.

For an ending, sit on the tape or hand it to someone. Hide it somewhere. Put it in your pocket and get your hand stuck. Put it in a paper bag and roll the bag up. Whatever you do, remember to take a big clown bow. Ta-da!

BE A CLOWN!

MAKING BALLOON ANIMALS

Tell your audience that you're going to make balloon animals. Take out a white rubber medical glove (you can usually get these at any pharmacy or drugstore), blow it up, and tie it at the wrist.

🖐 Show glove with the fingers facing up over clown kid's head (chicken).

🖐 Show glove with the fingers facing down under clown kid's chin (turkey).

🖐 Show glove out flat (spider).

🖐 Show glove in front of a clown kid with the fingers pointing down; kid pulling on the fingers (cow).

Note: It is very important to throw away popped or unused gloves in a covered trash can. They can be very dangerous for toddlers, little children, and pets, who might swallow them and choke. Please remember: Never leave them out in the open.

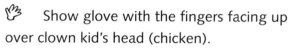

SWATTING AT MISCHIEVOUS MOSQUITOES

Like everyone else, clowns like to relax! So get comfy in a big easy chair with a good book and a cup of tea. Ah! That's the life. But wait … what's that buzzing around your head? You swat. Then you sip. *Bzzzzz.* You swat. Then, you turn a page. *Bzzzzz* again. You swat, then swat again. Now you're up out of the chair with arms and hands wildly flailing around your head. Now it's running up your sleeve; now it's on your head, making you quite itchy (lots of possibilities for pantomime with this one!).

All you need for this funny bit is your imagination and lots of exaggerated eye and head movements! For an ending, why not follow it around the stage, bent over or stretched up as you swat at it? Or you could lose it, ask for applause, and then be attacked by the buzzing once more. You could walk away and come back with a huge flyswatter to chase the fly offstage. Can you think of any other endings for your act?

SILLY SIGHT-&-SOUND GAGS!

Hat Flying off Your Head

Reach up with both hands to take off your hat and — whoosh — your hat flies up in the air. Every time you put it on — whoosh — it flies off again.

This trick is fun to do, but even more fun to watch! Hold the hat with one hand on each side of the brim. Make sure the second, fourth, and fifth fingers are on top of the brim. The third finger and thumb should be under the brim.

As you place the hat to your head, snap your second fingers up from your thumbs to propel the hat into the air. Whoosh — there goes your hat again, looking as if it's springing off your head every time you try to put it on.

You can do the same kind of trick with something you "accidentally" drop on the floor. As you bend down to pick it up, secretly kick it with your toe. As it moves, follow it and kick it a couple more times. You may have to jump on it to catch it! Perhaps you'll crush it when you do, which is good for a few outrageous facial expressions!

Stretching Your Thumb

Make a fist with your right hand and hold your thumb up. Grab the thumb with the left hand. As you do, place your left thumb between your second and third finger. (If you do this trick in front of a mirror, it will appear as if your right thumb is sticking up through the fingers on your left hand.) Slowly pull your left hand up to make it look as if you're stretching your thumb. Moan and groan, make lots of faces, and roll your eyes — basically, ham it up all you want!

— BE A CLOWN!

Sewing Your Fingers Together

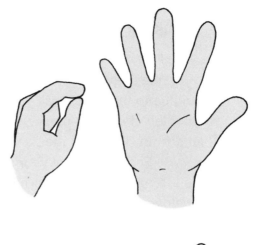

Pretend you're taking out a sewing needle and threading it. When you have the needle threaded, raise the hand that you're going to "sew," with the palm facing you and the back of the hand facing the audience. Starting from the bottom, push the needle through the side of your little finger (lots of grimacing expressions here!). Then pull the needle out the other side of the finger. Do the same with your fourth finger, then your third, your second, and finally your thumb until all of your fingers are sewn up (don't forget the grimaces!). As you pull the needle and thread, move your fingers together. When the fingers are all sewn together, push the needle through your shirt and pantomime seesawing your hand back and forth.

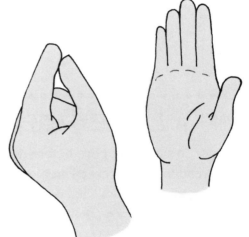

SILLY SIGHT-&-SOUND GAGS!

MAKING PUSH-BUTTON FACES

You'll have a good time practicing this funny bit in front of a mirror. Push your nose with one finger while you stick out your tongue. Pull your right cheek and move your tongue to the right. Push your nose again and move your tongue to the center. Pull your left cheek and move your tongue to the left. Continue these movements back and forth. Then pull the skin under your chin while you pull your tongue in.

Stick a finger in your right ear while you make a bulge in your left cheek with your tongue. Wiggle your finger while you wiggle your tongue inside your cheek. Remove your finger as you remove your tongue from your cheek. Try the other side. It's a simple bit, but very funny, and little kids love it! Big kids, too!

PULLING A LOOSE THREAD

The magic for this trick happens before the show. Put a spool of thread in your pocket Thread a needle with the thread from the spool. Poke the needle through your clothes so that it comes out on the outside of the clothing. Take the needle off and leave the thread hanging out.

When you're ready to perform this bit, find the loose thread on your costume and pull it out. It keeps coming … and coming … and coming … and coming. Your audience won't believe their eyes, and neither will you as you get tangled up in the thread!

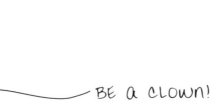

BE a CLOWN!

Index

Parents' Choice Approved
KIDS' ART WORKS!
Creating with Color, Design, Texture & More
by Sandi Henry

American Bookseller Pick of the Lists
Parents' Choice Honor Award
Benjamin Franklin Best Education/Teaching Book Award
2000 American Institute of Physics Science Writing Award
GIZMOS & GADGETS
Creating Science Contraptions that Work (& Knowing Why)
by Jill Frankel Hauser

American Bookseller Pick of the Lists
Parents' Choice Recommended
ADVENTURES IN ART
Arts & Crafts Experiences for 8- to 13-Year-Olds
by Susan Milord

Parents' Choice Gold Award
American Bookseller Pick of the Lists
Oppenheim Toy Portfolio Best Book Award
THE KIDS' MULTICULTURAL ART BOOK
Art & Craft Experiences from Around the World
by Alexandra M. Terzian

Selection of Book-of-the-Month; Scholastic Book Clubs
KIDS COOK!
Fabulous Food for the Whole Family
by Sarah Williamson & Zachary Williamson

The following *Kaleidoscope Kids*® books allow children, ages 7 to 13, to explore a subject from many different angles, using many different skills. All books are 96 pages, two-color, fully illustrated, 10 x 10, $10.95 US.

ANCIENT ROME!
Exploring the culture, people & ideas of this powerful empire
by Avery Hart

SKYSCRAPERS!
Super Structures to Design & Build
by Carol A. Johmann

WHO *REALLY* DISCOVERED AMERICA?
Unraveling the Mystery & Solving the Puzzle
by Avery Hart
American Bookseller Pick of the Lists
Children's Book Council Notable Book
Dr. Toy 10 Best Educational Products
PYRAMIDS!
50 Hands-On Activities to Experience Ancient Egypt
by Avery Hart & Paul Mantell

American Bookseller Pick of the Lists
Parent's Guide Children's Media Award
Children's Book Council Notable Book
Dr. Toy 100 Best Children's Products
KNIGHTS & CASTLES
50 Hands-On Activities to Experience the Middle Ages
by Avery Hart & Paul Mantell

American Bookseller Pick of the Lists
Parent's Guide Children's Media Award
ANCIENT GREECE!
40 Hands-On Activities to Experience This Wondrous Age
by Avery Hart & Paul Mantell

American Bookseller Pick of the Lists
MEXICO!
40 Activities to Experience Mexico Past and Present
by Susan Milord

GOING WEST!
Journey on a Wagon Train to Settle a Frontier Town
by Carol A. Johmann and Elizabeth J. Rieth

Prices may be slightly higher when purchased in Canada.

Visit Our Website!

To see what's new at Williamson, visit our website at:

www.williamsonbooks.com

To Order Books:

We accept Visa and MasterCard (*please include the number and expiration date*).

Toll-free phone orders with credit cards:

1-800-234-8791

Or, send a check with your order to:

**Williamson Publishing Company
P.O. Box 185
Charlotte, Vermont 05445**

*Please add **$4.00** for postage for one book plus **$1.00** for each additional book.
Satisfaction is guaranteed or full refund without questions or quibbles.*